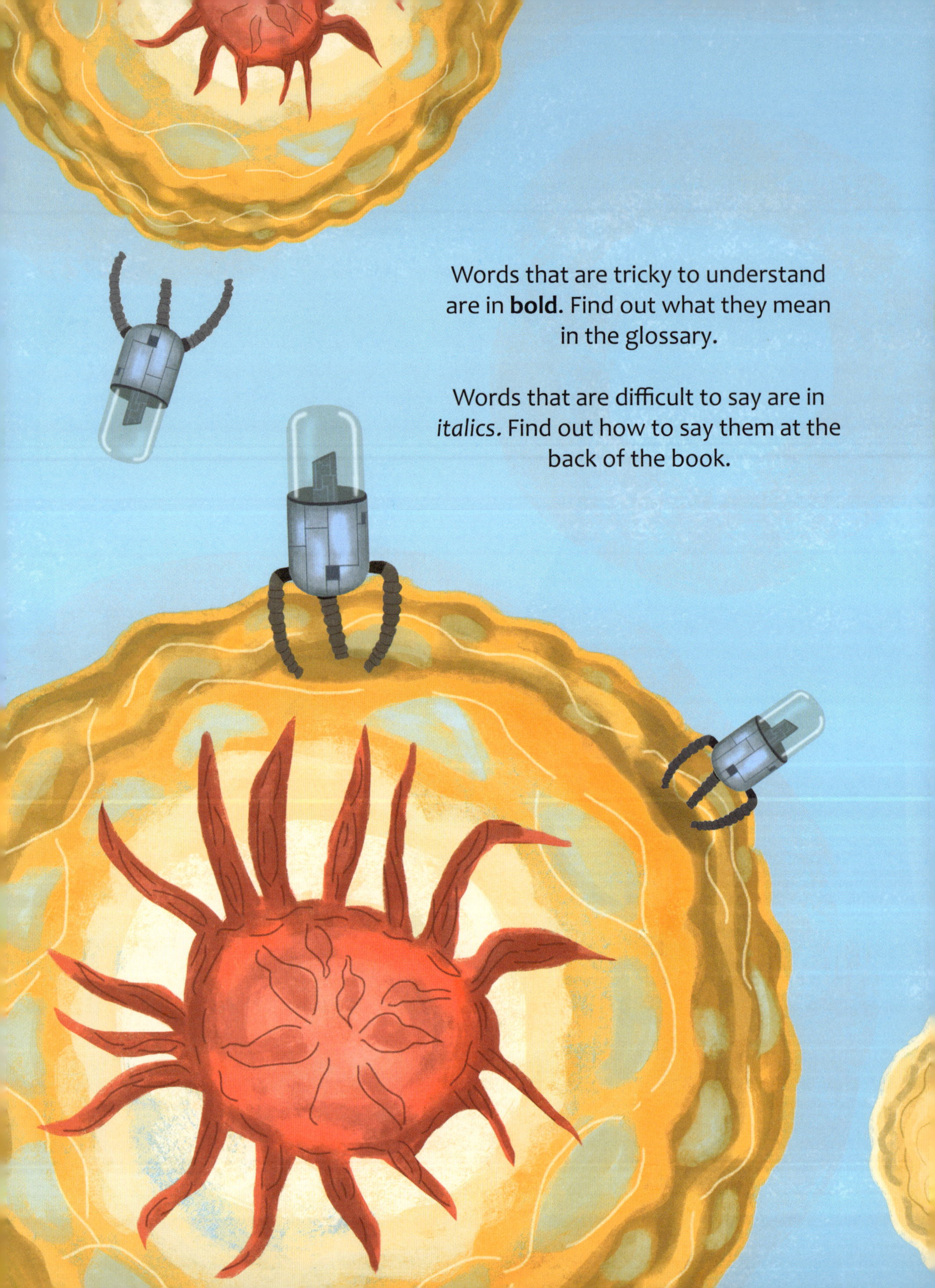

Words that are tricky to understand are in **bold**. Find out what they mean in the glossary.

Words that are difficult to say are in *italics*. Find out how to say them at the back of the book.

COULD GENES ALLOW US TO LIVE FOREVER?

DISCOVER THE SCIENCE BEHIND ***GENETICS***
(juh-NEH-ticks)

Written by Olivia Watson
Illustrated by Verónika Cháves Morales

WHAT IS GENETICS?

Genetics is the study of **genes**. It includes how genes vary to create differences in living things, as well as how **traits** are passed from one **generation** to the next.

The scientists who study genes are called **GENETICISTS.**

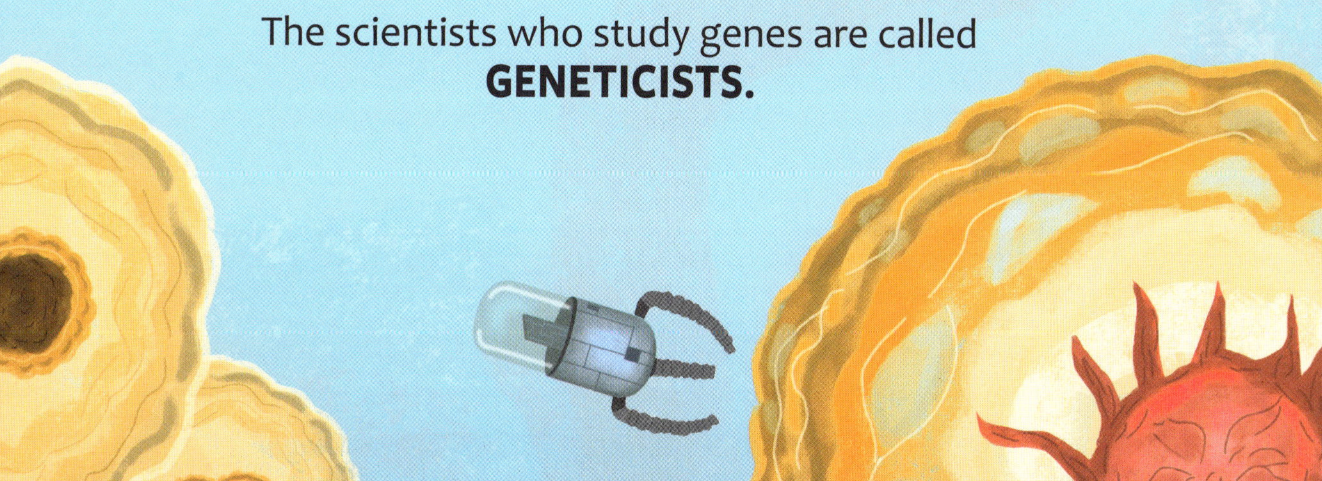

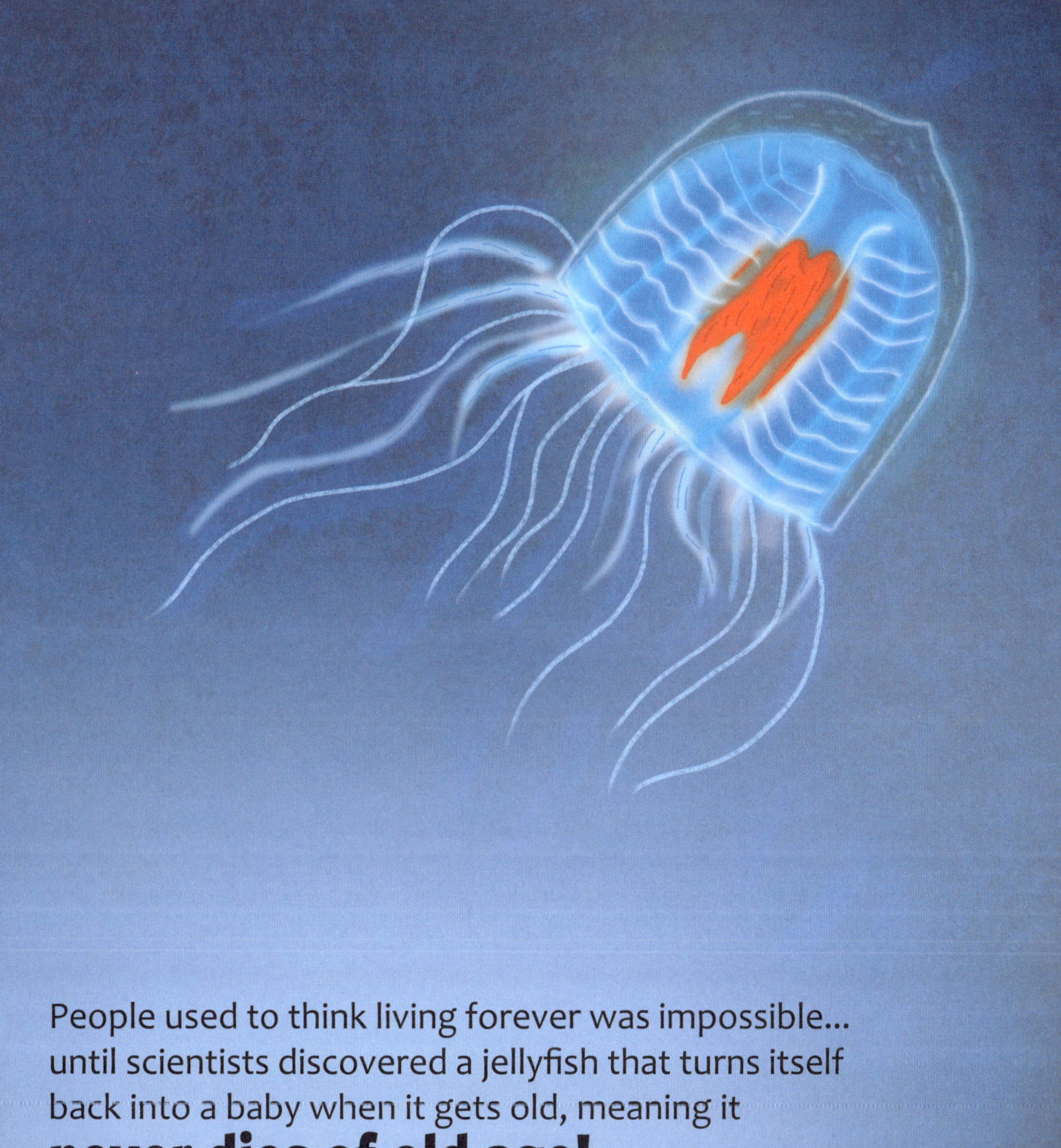

People used to think living forever was impossible... until scientists discovered a jellyfish that turns itself back into a baby when it gets old, meaning it

never dies of old age!

Scientists studied the jellyfish and figured out this ability comes from its genes. They're curious whether this discovery could help humans in some way too...

All living things have genes inside them, from insects and flowers to humans and bigger animals. Genes are like a set of instructions for how a living thing's body looks and works. They affect all sorts of things, like whether an animal has arms or wings, brown or blue eyes, or body features like...

Antlers
Wings
Beak
Petals
Leaves
Hooves

Humans have thousands of genes. They're so small they can't even be seen with a microscope! *Geneticists* used powerful tools to learn that genes are made of strands of **DNA**, which are

shaped like twisted ladders!

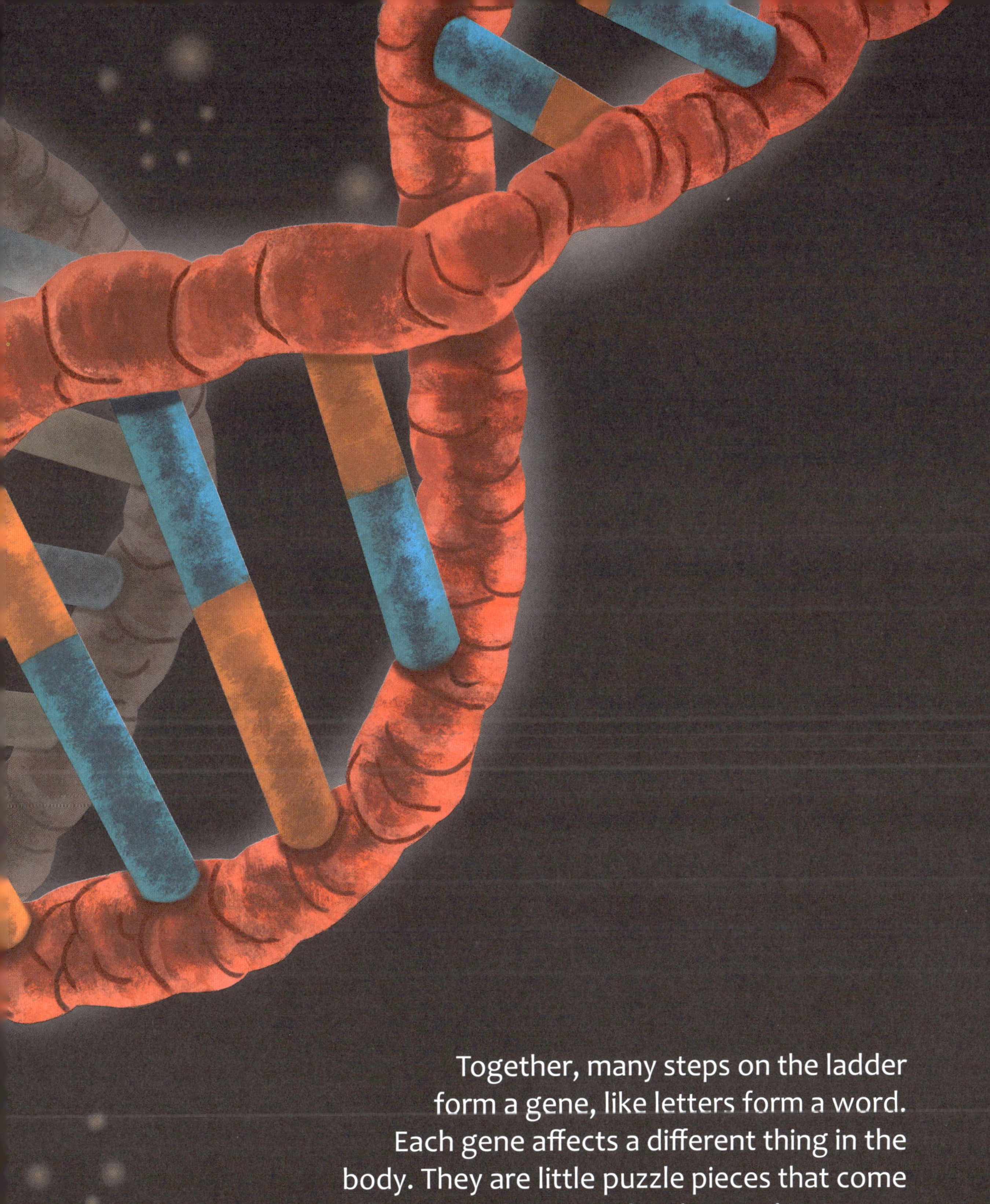

Together, many steps on the ladder form a gene, like letters form a word. Each gene affects a different thing in the body. They are little puzzle pieces that come from our parents and make us who we are.

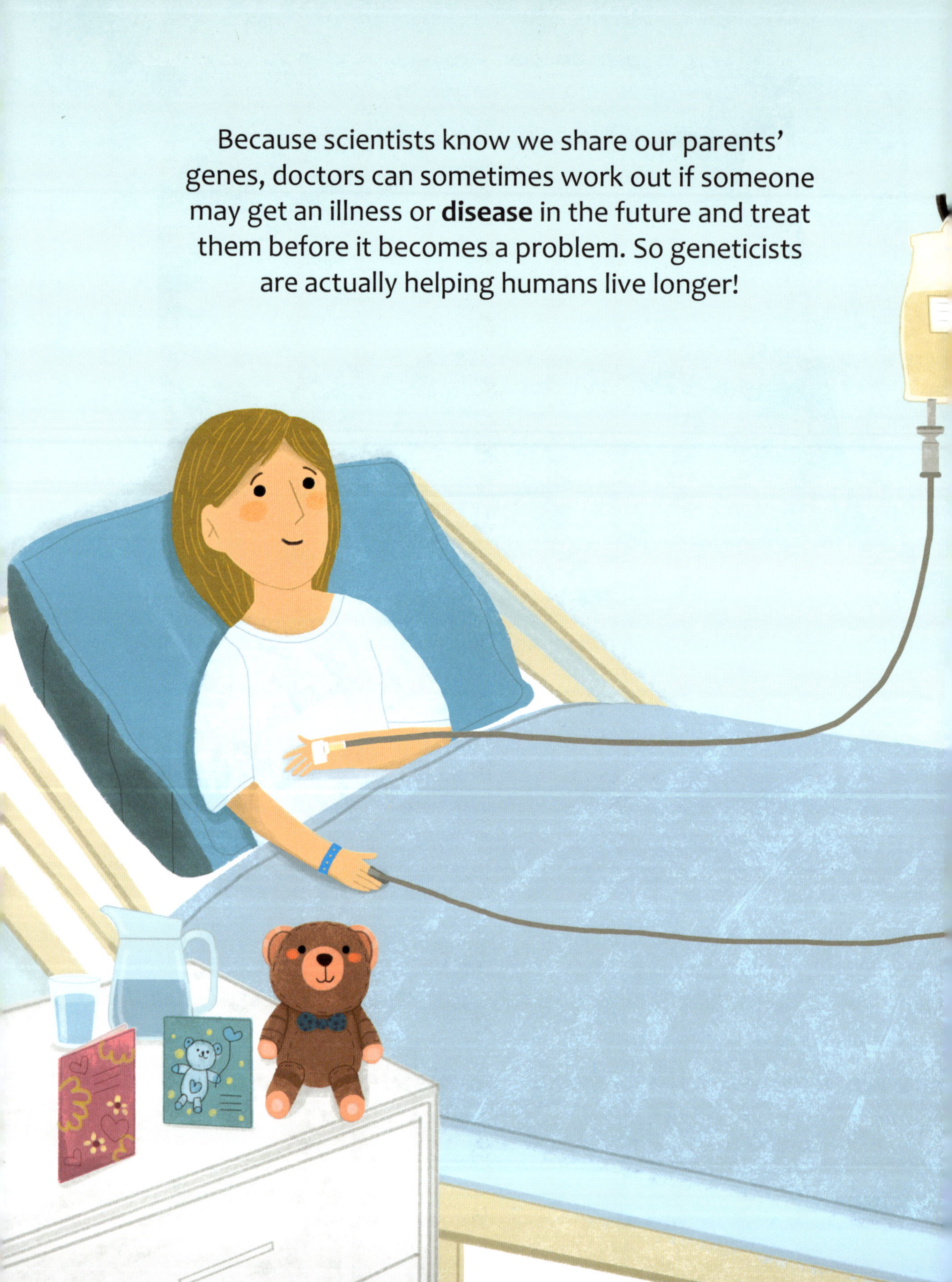

Because scientists know we share our parents' genes, doctors can sometimes work out if someone may get an illness or **disease** in the future and treat them before it becomes a problem. So geneticists are actually helping humans live longer!

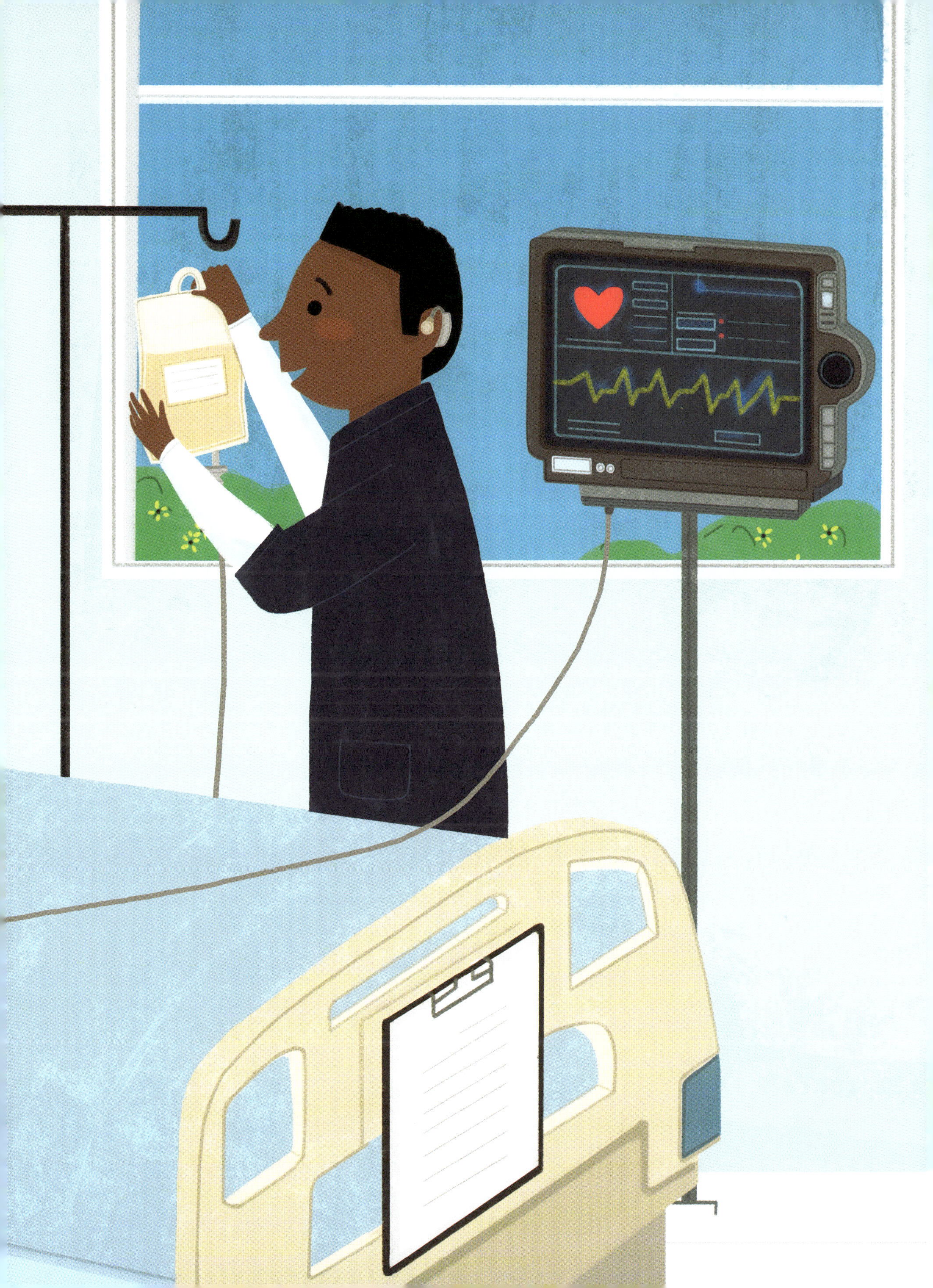

But geneticists don't just study humans, they learn about genes from animals too! Some elephants have a cancer-fighting gene that was **inactive** millions of years ago, but now protects them.

Scientists wonder if they could "turn off" harmful genes in humans, like the ones that cause illnesses, and "turn on" good ones that help keep people healthy.

Changing, or switching on and off, genes is complicated and some people think it could be done in the wrong way. But, scientists have succeeded at **modifying** cows' genes to make them **resistant** to **tuberculosis**. Cows used to pass this disease to humans and other animals, but not so much anymore. This has saved lots of lives!

While modifying animals' genes is a new process, changing **crops'** genes has been around for a while. Plants can be made resistant to harmful insects, like flies and caterpillars. This means farmers don't need to spray crops with strong **chemicals**, keeping soil and helpful insects, like bees, safer.

Plants can also be made to have more **vitamins** inside, making them healthier to eat…

and to grow in difficult conditions, like floods, helping them cope with **climate change**. Having lots of healthy food helps humans live longer.

Scientists are also exploring how to genetically modify **bacteria** to eat up waste like plastic. Plastic is really harmful – animals can get trapped in it and mistake pieces of it floating in the ocean for food. This is unhealthy for animals as it makes its way into the **food chain**. Plastic-eating bacteria could keep our natural world clean for all the things that call it home.

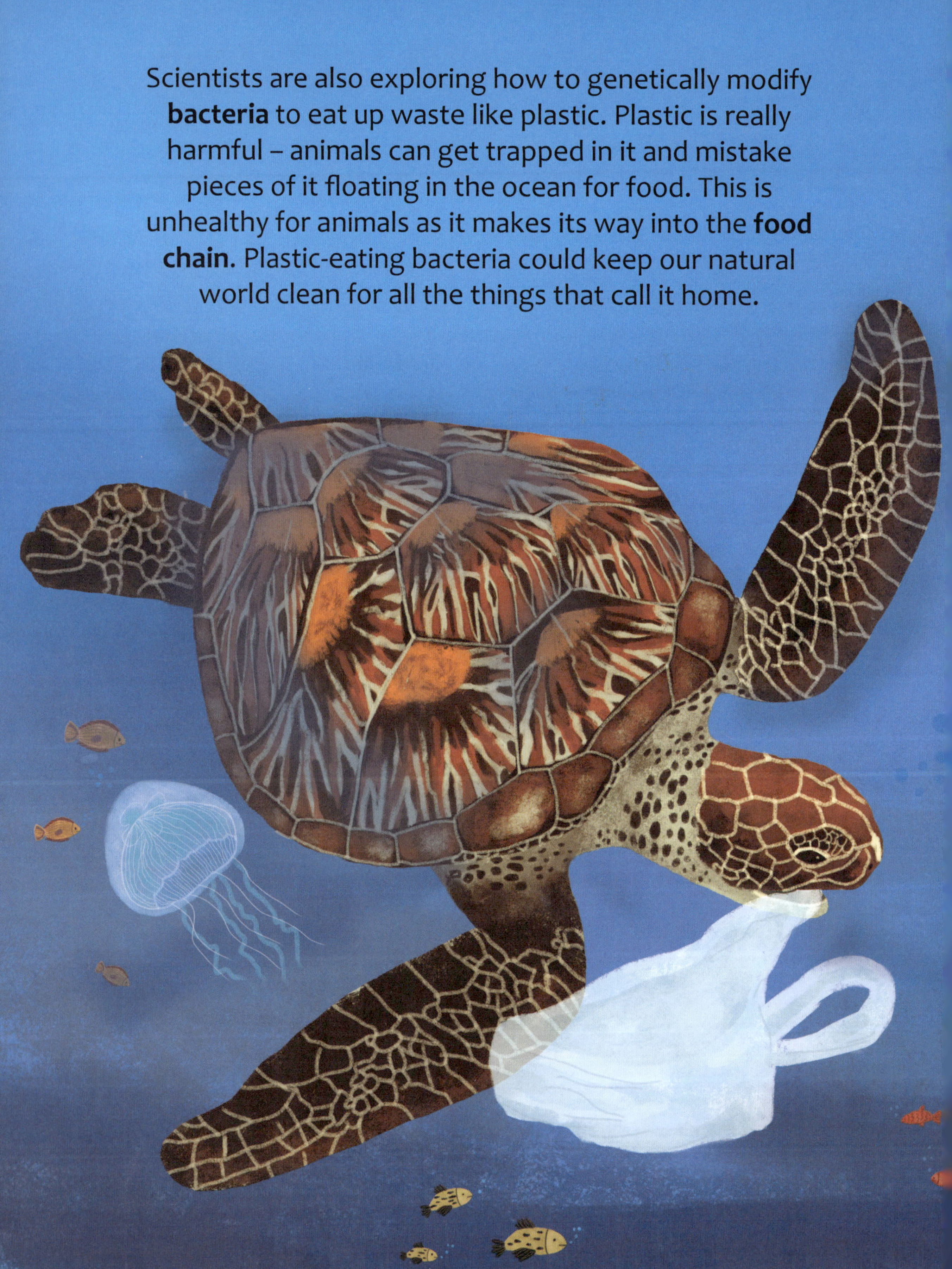

Genetics can make lives longer, but could it let us live forever? One of the biggest challenges is that, as we age, our **cells** and DNA become damaged and can't repair themselves anymore. This is where some animals shine...

The giant land tortoise has loads of genes that **protect and repair DNA!** They help it live for almost 200 years.

Tortoises aren't the only animals with genes that protect their DNA and cells from being damaged.

The naked mole rat's self-protecting genes allow it to age much slower and live much longer than other types of rats! But what do these discoveries mean for us?

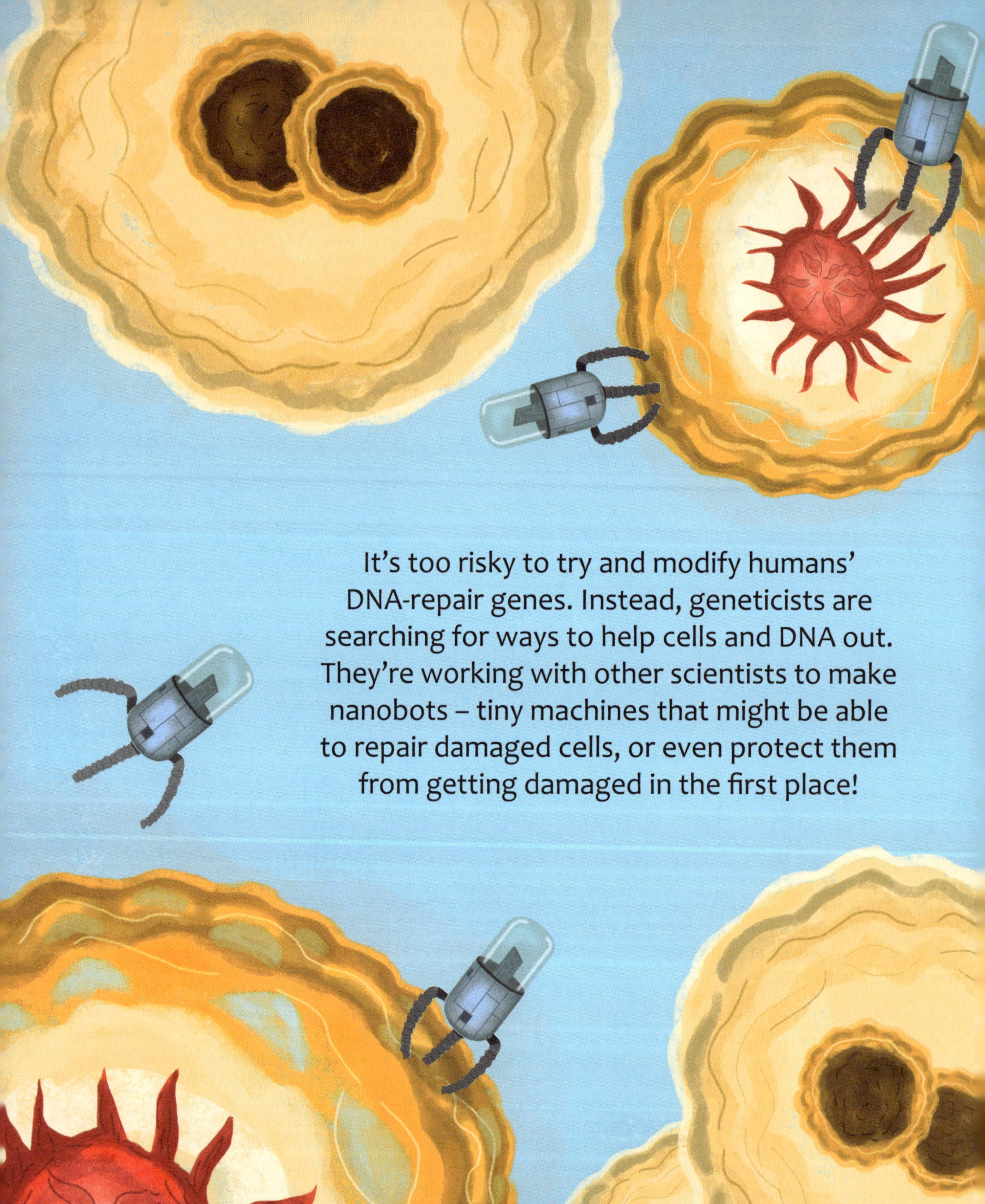

It's too risky to try and modify humans' DNA-repair genes. Instead, geneticists are searching for ways to help cells and DNA out. They're working with other scientists to make nanobots – tiny machines that might be able to repair damaged cells, or even protect them from getting damaged in the first place!

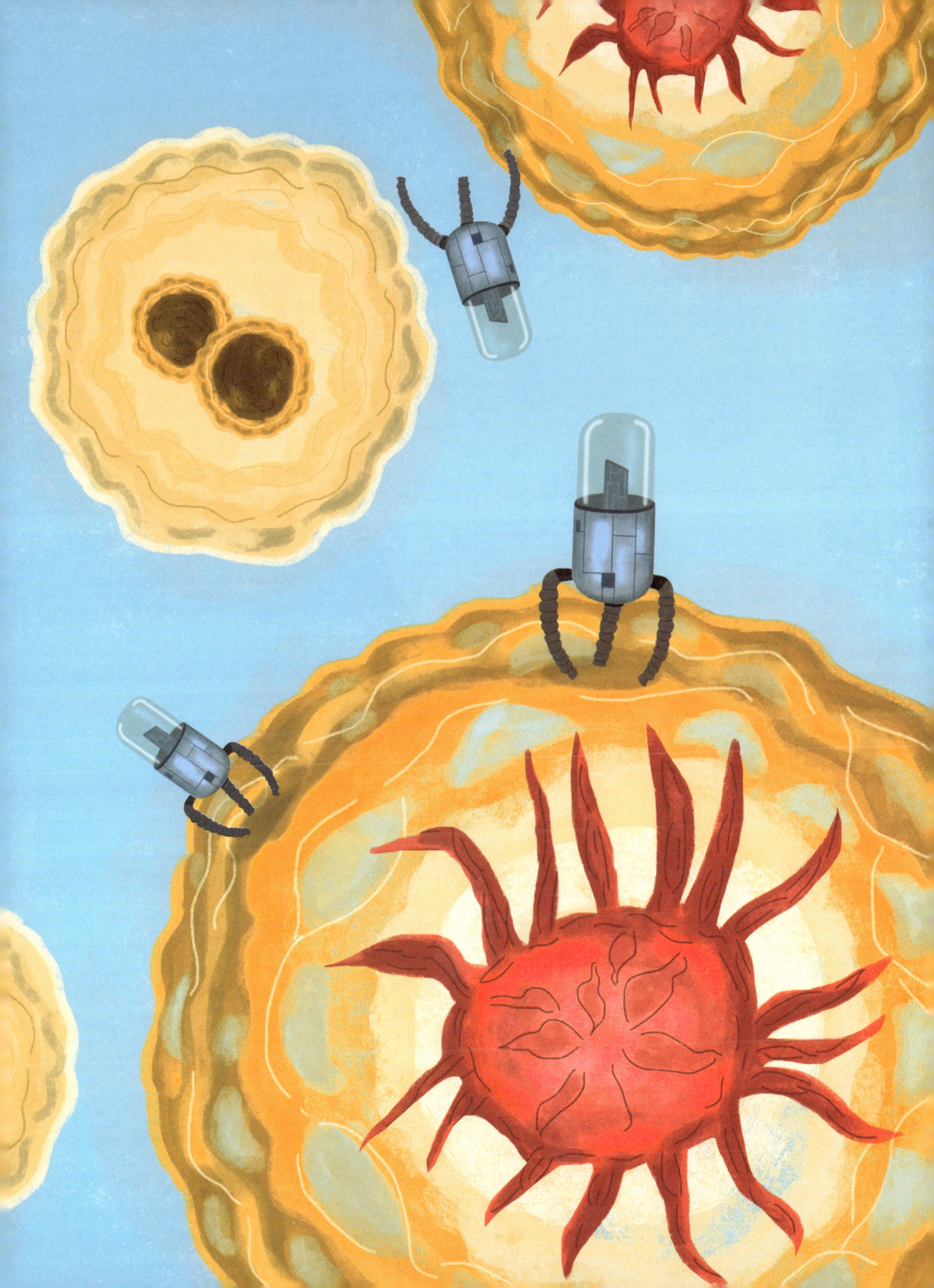

Some scientists think humans will never live past 150 years old, but our understanding of genetics is only just beginning. So far, geneticists have learned genes can help humans live longer and make the planet healthier too. With so many genes left to study and advances in technology, who knows what amazing discoveries lie ahead!

Maybe, one day soon mini-robots will
be able to change DNA!

While genetics don't tell the full story, they play an important part in understanding how some plants and animals live such long lives. And it's not just one gene, but lots of genes which makes this possible. Jellyfish aren't the only animals that live super long lives, there are plenty of record breakers in the animal kingdom, including...

Ocean quahog clam
Up to 500 years

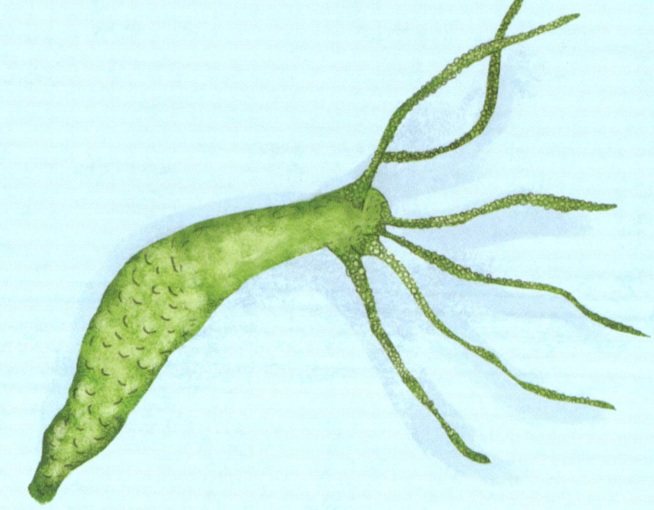

Hydra
May live forever

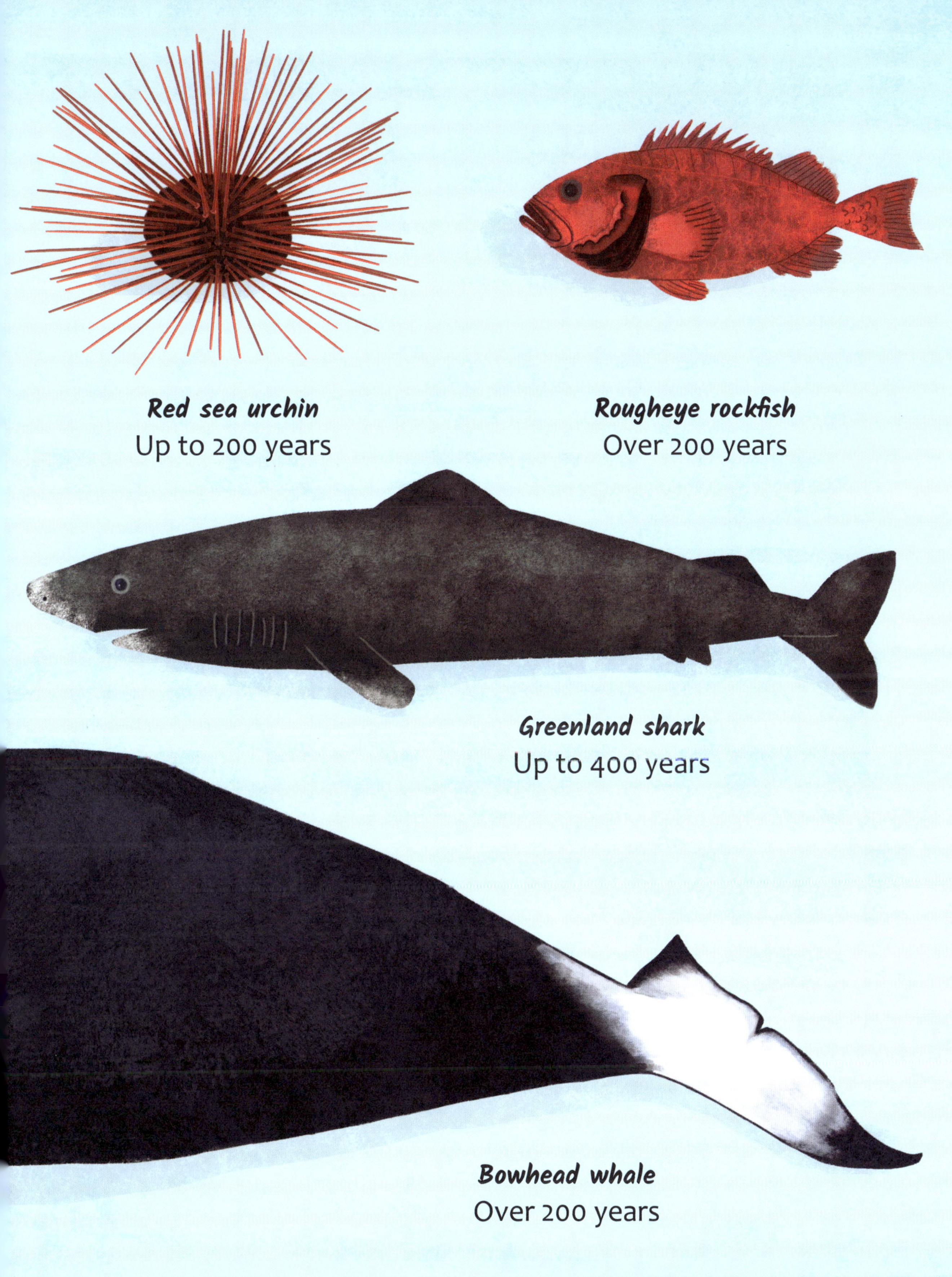
Red sea urchin
Up to 200 years
Rougheye rockfish
Over 200 years
Greenland shark
Up to 400 years
Bowhead whale
Over 200 years

Shortest-living

ANIMALS

Now we know all about animals that live long lives thanks to their genes, which animals live short lives because of their genes?

MAYFLIES

Mayflies spend most of their lives as babies that live in water. They only live as an adult for one day (or a few hours)! In their short time as an adult, they lay thousands of eggs.

HOUSEFLIES

These flies usually live for a month, but this can change depending on where they are. In hot places, their lives can be shorter, and in cooler places, they can be longer.

HONEY BEES

Scientists have noticed honey bees are living shorter lives now compared to 50 years ago. Research suggests this is to do with genetics, not the environment.

CICADAS

Some *cicadas* have unusual life cycles. After hatching from their eggs, they burrow underground where they live for up to 17 years. When they come out of the ground, they only live for four to six more weeks before dying!

PYGMY GOBY

Many of the shortest-living animals are insects, but not all. The *pygmy goby* fish only lives for two months. This means it holds the record for the shortest lifespan among **vertebrates**!

Groundbreaking

GENETICS FACTS

So, genes really do affect how long animals live, but what else is there to know? What else have geneticists discovered about genes?

HUMAN DNA IS REALLY LONG!

If you could stretch all the DNA in your body out into a straight line, it would stretch to the edge of the solar system and back... twice! But it would be so thin you wouldn't see it.

SOME ANIMALS CAN MODIFY THEIR OWN GENES!

Scientists have discovered that octopuses and squid modify their genes to make their bodies better at coping with changes to water temperature.

GENES AFFECT ALL SORTS OF THINGS!

It's not just how long you live – genes also affect your appearance, hobbies, and personality. But they don't have complete control; how you've been raised and who you spend time with matter too.

ALMOST EVERYONE'S DNA IS UNIQUE!

Humans share 99.9% of their DNA, but it's that tiny 0.1% that makes up all our differences. That means everyone's combination of DNA is **unique**. The only exception is identical twins who have the exact same DNA.

SOME PEOPLE'S GENES CHANGE OVER TIME!

Genes can change for people who spend time in extreme environments, like mountain climbers, scuba divers, and astronauts!

GLOSSARY

Bacteria – tiny living things that can be found in all natural environments.

Cells – tiny parts that make up all living things. Each cell has a different job to keep the body working properly.

Chemicals – substances made up of the same tiny building blocks. They are often made by humans.

Climate change – a change in the weather conditions over a long time.

Crops – plants that are grown in large quantities to feed people.

Disease – a medical condition that causes part of a living thing to no longer work properly.

DNA – a unique code inside every living thing that tells it how to grow and build itself. DNA is made up of genes.

Food chain – the order in which different animals eat each other to survive.

Generation – a group of people born around the same time.

Genes – tiny instructions inside living things that make up DNA (see above). Genes affect how a living thing looks and how its body works. *Need help saying this? Look below!*

Inactive – something that is not currently working.

Modifying – changing something for a specific reason.

Resistant – to no longer be affected by something.

Traits – physical features, characteristics, and ways people tend to act.

Tuberculosis – a disease (see left) that affects a living thing's lungs. *Need help saying this? Look below!*

Unique – something that is one of its kind; unlike all others.

Vertebrates – animals that have a backbone inside their body.

Vitamins – substances that are needed to keep a body healthy. Humans get most of their vitamins from food.

HOW DO I SAY?

Cicadas
sih-KAH-duh-z

Genes
JEEN-z

Geneticists
juh-NEH-tih-sists

Genetics
juh-NEH-ticks

Pygmy goby
pig-me go-bee

Quahog
coh-hog

Tuberculosis
too-ber-cue-loh-sis

THE BIG QUESTIONS ANSWERED

This is more than just a series of books; it is a complete resource. Accompanying each book is a variety of FREE material to engage curious kids with science.

www.thebigquestionsanswered.com

Use the QR code to visit the website, download free resources, and discover other books in the series.

On the website, find out incredible things about geneticists, including what they do, some of their greatest discoveries, and the people who have made a difference in this field of science.

The material is also available for home or classroom use, supporting all the information in this book.

Teachers' & Parents' Resources
With discussion prompts and questions, extra information, and facts around key topics.

Young Geneticists' Activity Pack
Fun activities for wannabe genes experts, including creative writing, drawing, word searches, and much, much more.

The Big Questions Answered is published by Beetle Books. Beetle Books is an imprint of Hungry Tomato Ltd.

First published in 2025 by Hungry Tomato Ltd
F15, Old Bakery Studios, Blewetts Wharf, Malpas Road, Truro, Cornwall, TR1 1QH, UK.

ISBN 9781835691441

A CIP catalog record for this book is available from the British Library.

With thanks to:
Editors: Holly Thornton and Millie Burdett
Designers: Amy Harvey and Meg Holbrook
The team at Beehive Illustration
Consultant: Professor Michael Cant

Information in this book is up to date as of the time of writing.

Printed and bound in China.

Picture Credits:
(t = top, b = bottom, m = middle, l = left, r = right)
Shutterstock: Alex Terentii 34mr; balein 35mr; bt_photo 32ml; dreamnikon 33ml; irin-k 33tr; Kondratuk Aleksei 34bl; matimix 35tl; m.mphoto 35bl; Pavaphon Supanantananont 33br; Rudmer Zwerver 32br.